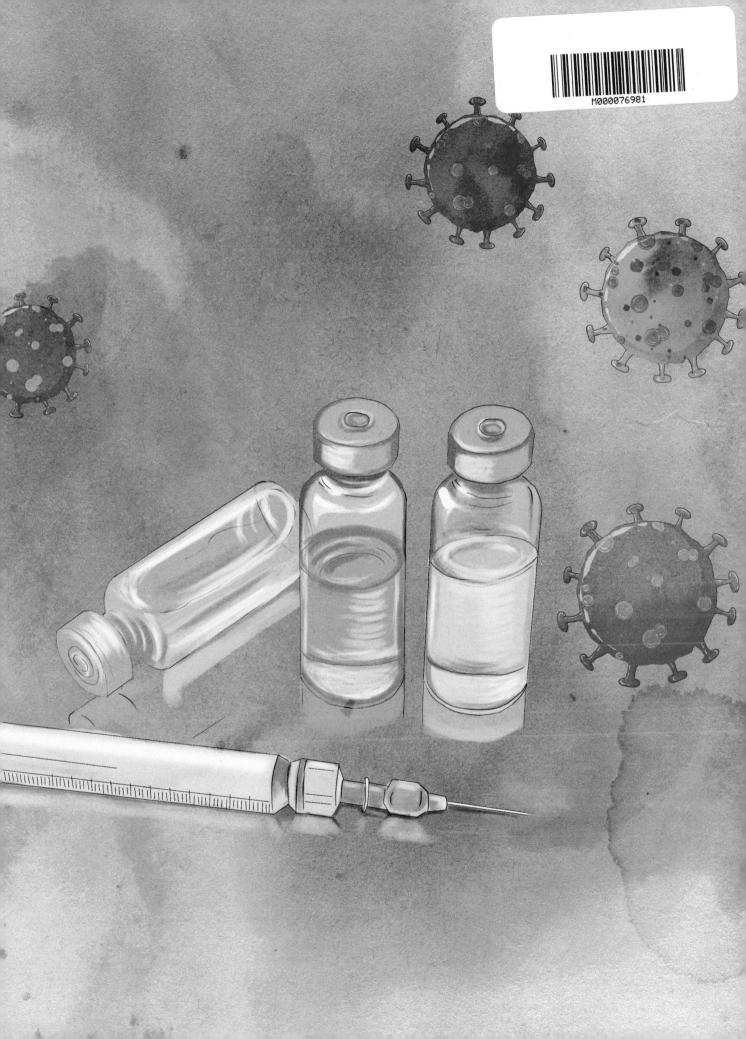

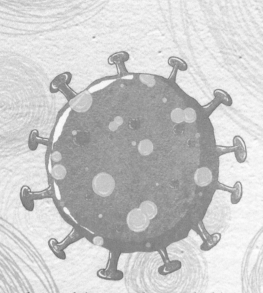

Vaccines Explained (Spanish-English)
Text Copyright © 2021 Ohemaa Boahemaa
Illustrations Copyright © 2021 Joyeeta Neogi
Published by Language Lizard
Basking Ridge, NJ 07920
info@LanguageLizard.com

Visit us at www.LanguageLizard.com

First edition 2021

Library of Congress Control Number: 2021903332

ISBN: 978-1-63685-056-6 (Print)
ISBN: 978-1-63685-057-3 (eBook)

TODO SOBRE LAS VACUNAS
VACCINES EXPLAINED

(Español - Inglés)
(Spanish - English)

BY OHEMAA BOAHEMAA

ILLUSTRATED BY JOYEETA NEOGI

TRANSLATED BY GEOVANNA DELGADO

Language Lizard
Basking Ridge

La mayoría de los medicamentos ayudan a que el cuerpo se mejore cuando una persona está enferma. Las **vacunas** son un tipo especial de medicamento que ayudan al cuerpo a no enfermarse.

Most medicines help the body get better when a person is sick. **Vaccines** are a special kind of medicine that help the body to not get sick.

Nos enfermamos cuando gérmenes malos, generalmente **virus** o **bacterias**, entran a nuestro cuerpo. Estos gérmenes nos **infectan**, convirtiendo nuestro cuerpo en una fábrica de gérmenes.

We get sick when bad germs, usually **viruses** or **bacteria**, enter our body. These germs **infect** us, turning our body into a germ factory.

Cómo los virus pueden infectar el cuerpo:
How viruses can infect the body:

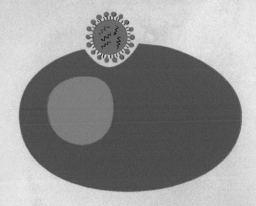

El virus entra a la **célula**.

Virus enters **cell**.

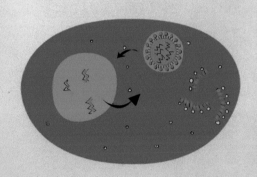

La célula produce más virus.

Cell makes more viruses.

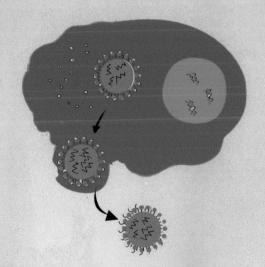

Los nuevos virus destruyen a la célula y se van.

New viruses destroy cell and leave.

Las vacunas tienen dentro de ellas pedacitos de gérmenes. Ellas se encargan de enseñarle a nuestro cuerpo a combatir a ese germen. Cuando ese germen entra en una persona que ya ha sido vacunada, su cuerpo es capaz de destruirlo. Esto evita que la persona se enferme.

Vaccines have little pieces of germs in them. They work by teaching our body to fight that germ. When that germ enters a person who has already had the vaccine, the body can destroy it. This stops the person from getting sick.

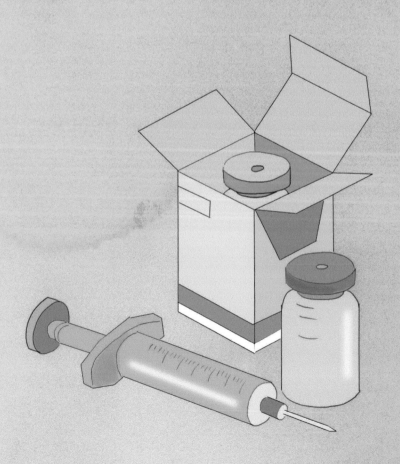

La ciencia de las vacunas comenzó hace cientos de años cuando los doctores descubrieron que algunas personas no se enfermaban aun cuando tenían un germen malo. Estas personas eran **inmunes** a ciertas enfermedades.

The science of vaccines started hundreds of years ago when doctors discovered that some people did not become sick, even when they got a bad germ. These people were **immune** to certain illnesses.

Los científicos descubrieron que podían crear medicamentos que generaban inmunidad en las personas. Estos medicamentos, llamados vacunas, evitarían que las personas se enfermaran.

Scientists figured out that they could make medicines that created immunity in people. These medicines, called vaccines, would stop people from getting sick.

La poliomielitis fue una enfermedad terrible que lastimó y mató a mucha gente. En 1953, un científico llamado Jonas Salk creó la vacuna para la poliomielitis. Esta fue una de las primeras vacunas usadas alrededor del mundo.

Polio was a terrible illness that hurt and killed many people. In 1953, a scientist named Jonas Salk created a vaccine for polio. This was one of the first vaccines to be used all around the world.

Hoy en día tenemos vacunas que previenen diferentes enfermedades. En gran medida, ponerte una vacuna evitará que contraigas la enfermedad. Sin embargo, si te enfermas, la vacuna evitará que te enfermes seriamente.

We now have vaccines that prevent many different illnesses. Most of the time, getting a vaccine will stop you from getting that illness. However, if you do get sick, the vaccine stops you from getting very sick.

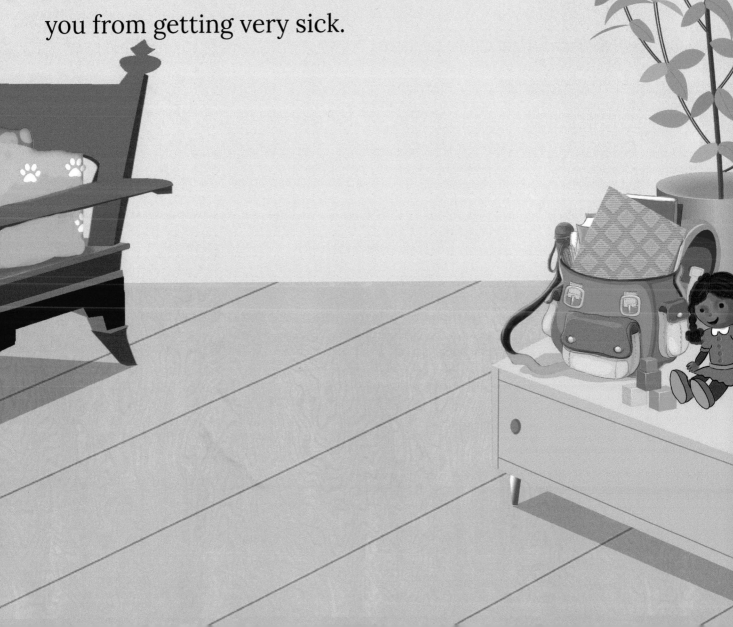

Las vacunas han ayudado a eliminar del mundo muchas enfermedades peligrosas como la viruela y el sarampión. A medida que nuevas enfermedades surgen, los científicos trabajan para crear nuevas vacunas para ellas.

Vaccines have helped to get rid of dangerous illnesses, including smallpox and measles, from much of the world. As new illnesses develop, scientists work to create vaccines for them.

La mayoría de las vacunas son aplicadas mediante una inyección en el consultorio del doctor o en una farmacia. ¡Esto puede parecer aterrador, pero es rápido y fácil!

Most vaccines are given as a shot, which can be given at a doctor's office or pharmacy. This might seem scary, but it is quick and easy!

¡Hasta tenemos vacunas para nuestros animales!

We even have vaccines for our animals!

Personas de todas las edades pueden ser vacunadas. Las vacunas son una forma importante de mantener saludable a todos en el mundo.

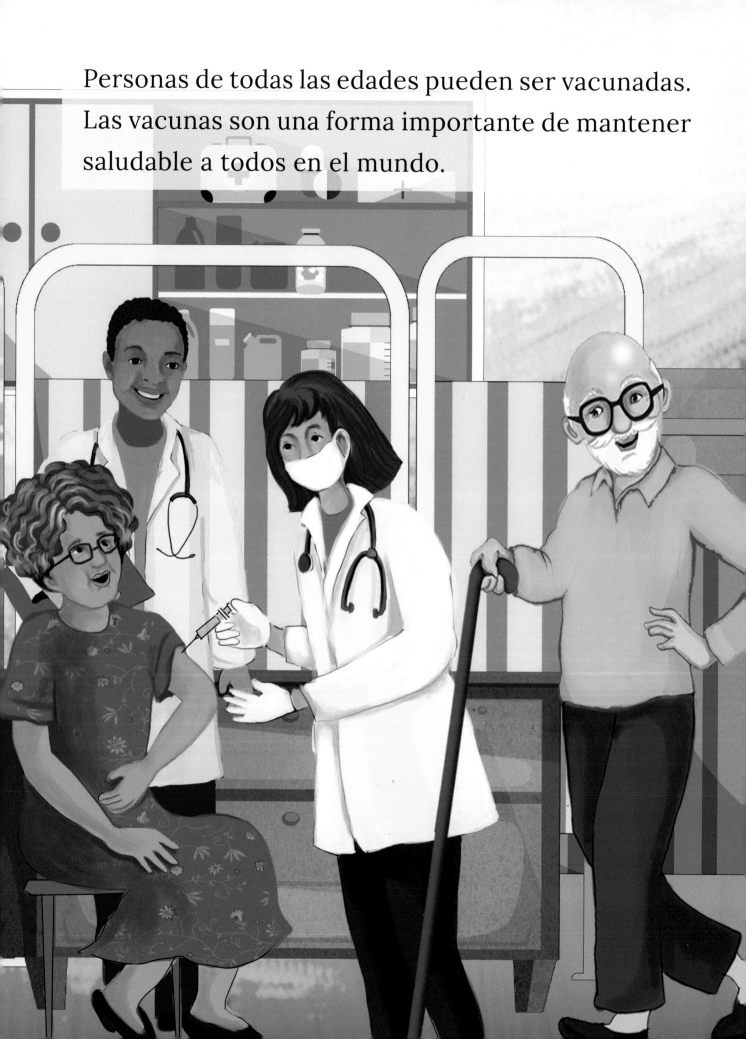

People of all ages can get vaccinated.
Vaccines are an important way of keeping
the world healthy.

Palabras importantes que debemos conocer:

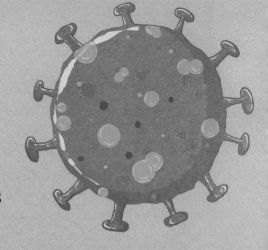

Bacteria: es un tipo de germen. Algunas bacterias pueden hacer que nuestro cuerpo enferme.

Célula: es la unidad fundamental del cuerpo humano. Tu cuerpo está formado por millones de células.

Inmune: una persona inmune no se enferma aun cuando entre un germen malo a su cuerpo.

Infectar: es cuando un germen malo entra al cuerpo y detiene el trabajo normal del cuerpo.

Vacuna: es un tipo de medicamento que ayuda al cuerpo a no enfermarse.

Virus: es un tipo de germen malo que hace que nuestro cuerpo se enferme.

Important words to know:

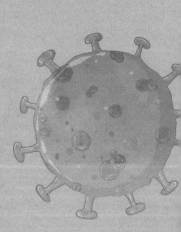

Bacteria: A type of germ. Some bacteria can make our body sick.

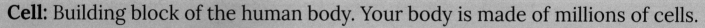

Cell: Building block of the human body. Your body is made of millions of cells.

Immune: An immune person doesn't get sick even if a bad germ enters their body.

Infect: When a bad germ enters the body and stops the body's normal work.

Vaccine: A kind of medicine that helps the body to not get sick.

Virus: A type of bad germ that makes our body sick.

For audio and teacher resources, including a lesson plan about vaccines, scan this code or go to: *https://www.LanguageLizard.com/Vaccine*

Want to learn more?

These websites have additional information about vaccines:

- **World Health Organization (WHO):**

    https://www.who.int/

- **Gates Foundation:**

    https://www.gatesfoundation.org/

- **US Centers for Disease Control:**

    https://www.cdc.gov/

- **European Centre for Disease Prevention and Control (ECDC):** *https://www.ecdc.europa.eu/en*

- **Africa CDC:** *https://africacdc.org/*

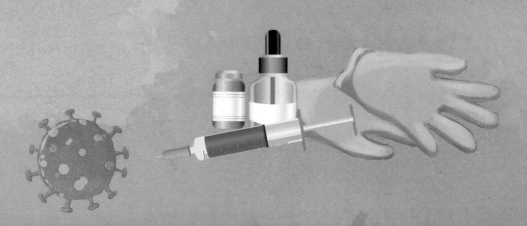

About the author:

Ohemaa Boahemaa is from Ghana and grew up in South Africa and the United States. She has loved science since she was a little girl and studied cellular and molecular biomedical sciences at Johns Hopkins University and Columbia University. She currently works at the Rutgers School of Public Health, planning classes that bring together students from around the world to learn about keeping each other healthy.

About the illustrator:

Joyeeta Neogi has been working as an illustrator for over ten years, using both traditional and digital mediums. Her colorful, playful style brings picture books to life. She studied at Northern India Institute of Fashion Technology and currently resides in Bangalore, India. Joyeeta also illustrated *Icing on the Cake: Food Idioms*, part of Language Lizard's Idiom book series.